MY SUCCESS TRADING JOURNAL

ISBN #: 978-0-578-78761-9 (paperback)

Published by LGC Publishing (lgcpublishing.com)

Design by HypeHer™ Ventures (hypeherventures.com)

Please refer all pertinent questions to lifeguidecoaches@gmail.com.

AUTHOR'S DISCLAIMER

Before investing and taking ANY trade in the foreign exchange market, you should carefully consider:

1. Your investment objectives
2. Your Level of experience
3. Your Risk appetite.

There is a possibility that you could sustain loss of some or all of your initial investment, so you should NOT invest money you can't afford to lose. You should be aware of all the risks associated with Foreign Exchange Trading and seek advice from an Independent Financial Advisor if you have any doubts.

PAST PERFORMANCES ARE NOT INDICATIVE OF FUTURE RESULTS!

While attempts have been made to verify the accuracy of information provided in this journal, neither the author nor the publisher assumes responsibility for errors, inaccuracies, or omissions. Information contained in this journal is provided for the sole purpose of assisting Beginner Traders with important trading information available at their finger-tips. There are no claims by the Author, Life Guide Coaches, LLC or any of its employees, and affiliates that the trading strategies or methodologies in this journal will result in profits and will not result in losses. This journal does not guarantee to produce profits.

Foreign Currency trading on FOREX and trading results in general vary from individual to individual and may not be suitable for everyone. Any opinions, strategies, techniques, methodologies, research, analysis, prices, or other information contained in this journal are provided as general market commentary, for educational purposes only, and does not constitute investment advice or a solicitation to buy or sell any Forex contract or securities of any type.

Life Guide Coaches, LLC or any of its employees, will not accept liability for any loss or damage, including without limitation any loss of profit, which may arise directly or indirectly from use of or reliance on such information. You agree to use this journal and the information contained within at your own risk. By using this journal, you confirm your agreement with the terms above, confirm and exempt the author, publisher, and company, from any liabilities or litigation.

TABLE OF CONTENTS

COACHING CORNER

WINNER GUIDES

PIP TALKS

TABLE OF CONTENTS

SUCCESS TRADING

WINNER'S INVITATION

COACHING

CORNER

STARTS HERE

INVEST

YOUR MONEY IN

FOREIGN

TRADE

AND ONE OF THESE DAYS

YOU WILL

MAKE A

PROFIT

ECCLESIASTES 11:1

(GOOD NEWS TRANSLATION)

DONNA'S MEMO

This journal was created by a Beginner Trader who understands how exciting, yet overwhelming it can be to dive in and "earn while you learn".

Forex Trading is a profitable skill. In this business, strategy is key! I created the *My Success Trading Journal* with you in mind to make the discipline of keeping a detailed log of your trades **simple.** This one-of-a-kind tool compiles several helpful, and pertinent resources necessary for successful trading.

Every trader's goal is to take profit, leverage losses and enjoy Blue Skies. My hope is that while we learn, and take this mission together, you will gain momentum, build revenue, and begin to see what I call "profit-*ability*". There are no limits! May you experience C.A.V.U. – Ceiling And Visibility Unlimited – as you use your new skill-set to rise above lack and soar on to blue skies of continual wealth, and increase.

A Special Thank You To:

My Financial Mentor, *Dr. Mary House* & Brickhouse Trading Group

My Team Lead, *Increase Coach* Teresa Tate of Blue Skies Trading Group

My Husband & Life Business Partner *Mr. Blue Skies*,

Pastor Robert L. Edward, Jr.

I appreciate ALL of your support and encouragement with this project!

Your Winner's Coach,
Rev. Donna Edward

JOURNAL GUIDE

A Tool for Beginner Traders

Learning to trade can be challenging, and for some it can be a little over-whelming. While many give up before they have the chance to really get started, countless beginner traders really want a coach, and a tool; something to guide us along the way. The official ***My Success Trading Journal*** uses several of the foundational resources that helped take the fear out of trading and motivated me to get started while enriching my experience.

I am convinced that this tool is the one so many of us have been waiting for. In it you will find inspiration, wisdom, affirmations, key trading terms, including sections dedicated to helping you understand several topics necessary for beginner traders. Best of all, it offers the space to track your trades (demo & live) and discover potential winning strategies.

I want you to use it as a guide while you're developing your new skill-set.

Here's How

Start with the ***Winner Guides*** and go through each section without skipping a page. Take the time to read through the ***Trading Terms***, ***Market Necessities***, ***Trade Nuggets***, ***Trading Plan***, ***PIP Counter***, and Profit-Ability Sheet.

Special Note

Success Trading is the heart of this journal. Our proprietary ***Demo Trade Trackers & Live Trade Trackers*** were created to help you build "trade confidence". I'm giving you one hundred ***Trade Trackers*** (20 ***Demo Trade Trackers***, and 80 ***Live Trade Trackers*** total). For every ten trackers, there is one ***Demo/ Live Reflection*** sheet for you to recall/record video notes, team notes, your biggest win and a teachable moment. I even included extra sheets of note paper to reduce the need to purchase additional notebooks.

The journal concludes with a list of valuable trade resources, and an invitation to join the *Blue Skies Trading Group.*

I hope you enjoy this tool so much that you share it with your trading friends! Email winnerscoach.dme@gmail.com if you are interested in purchasing bulk quantities.

WINNER

GUIDES

START HERE

JUST FOR YOU

Welcome to the Winner's Circle.
Below you will find a few
principles we live by

1

WINNING IS A DECISION

2

BE INTENTIONAL

3

NOTHING BEATS
CONSISTENCY

4

WE DON'T RUSH
OUR PROCESS

GOAL KEEPER

Use this sheet to record five trading goals you will set for your beginner's journey. Be sure to record each achievement date.

1

Achievement Date

2

Achievement Date

3

Achievement Date

4

Achievement Date

5

Achievement Date

WINNER'S CREED

Repeat After Me

I am a successful Forex Trader.

I am a life-learning student of wealth.

The world is my classroom.

I will use each of my tools to practice successful trading.

I will not compare my success to anyone else.

My wins will outweigh my losses.

I'm always a winner.

I win to trade another day.

Forex Trading is for me!

TRADING CREED

A creed is a set of beliefs which guides someone's actions. Take time to create a list of *Trading Creeds* that you will use to guide the development of your new skill-set.

1

2

3

4

5

TRADING TERMS

A

ACCRUAL

The apportionment of premiums and discounts on forward exchange transactions that relate directly to deposit swap (interest arbitrage) deals, over the period of each deal.

ADJUSTMENT

Official action normally occasioned by a change either in the internal economic policies to correct a payment imbalance or in the official currency rate.

B

BAR CURRENCY

The first currency in a currency pair. It shows how much the base currency is worth as measured against the second currency. For example, if the USD/CHF (U.S. Dollar/Swiss Franc) rate equals 1.6215, then one USD is worth CHF 1.6215. In the forex market, the US dollar is normally considered the base currency for quotes, meaning that quotes are expressed as a unit of $1 USD per the other currency quoted in the pair. The primary exceptions to this rule are the British pound, the euro and the Australian dollar.

BEARISH/BEAR MARKET

The market is moving in a downward direction favoring a declining market and rising prices. For example, "We are bearish EUR/USD" means that we think the euro will weaken against the dollar.

BID/ASK SPREAD

The difference between the bid and the ask (offer) price.

BID PRICE

The price at which the market is prepared to buy a product. Prices are quoted two-way as Bid/Ask. In FX trading, the Bid represents the price at which a trader can sell the base currency, shown to the left in a currency pair. For example, in the quote USD/CHF 1.4527/32, the base currency is USD, and the Bid price is 1.4527, meaning you can sell one US Dollar for 1.4527 Swiss francs.

BROKER

An individual or firm that acts as an intermediary, bringing buyers and sellers together for a fee or commission.

BULLISH/BULL MARKET

The market is moving in an upward direction favoring a strengthening market. For example, "We are bullish EUR/USD" means that we think the euro will strengthen against the dollar.

BOLLINGER BANDS (BB)

A tool used by technical analysts. A band plotted two standard deviations on either side of a simple moving average, which often indicates support and resistance levels.

C

CANDLESTICK CHART

A chart that indicates the trading range for the day as well as the opening and closing price. If the open price is higher than the close price, the rectangle between the open and close price is shaded. If the close price is higher than the open price, that area of the chart is not shaded.

CONSOLIDATION

A period of range-bound activity after an extended price move when the market is moving sideways.

CURRENCIES

AUD: Australian Dollar

CAD: Canadian Dollar

CHF: Swiss Franc

CNY: Chinese Renminbi (Yuan)

EUR: European Dollar

GBP: British Pound

HKD: Hong Kong Dollar

JPY: Japanese Yen

KRW: South Korean Won

NZD: New Zealand Dollar

USD: U.S. Dollar

XAG: Silver

XAU: Gold

XPD: Palladium

XPT: Platinum

CURRENCY PAIRS

Currencies are always traded in pairs. The most common (major) are:

* AUD/USD	* USD/CHF
* EUR/USD	* USD/CAD
* EUR/GBP	USD/CNY
* GBP/USD	USD/HKD
* USD/JPY	USD/KRW

TRADING TERMS

M

MARGIN

The required equity that an investor must deposit to collateralize a position.

O

OFFER

The rate at which a dealer is willing to sell a currency.

P

PIPS

Short for Points In Percentage. It is a standard of measuring the movement in the Forex Market.

Q

QUOTE

An indicative market price, normally used for information purposes only.

R

RATE

An indicative market price, normally used for information purposes only.

RESISTANCE

A term used in technical analysis indicating a specific price level at which analysis concludes people will sell.

RISK

Exposure to uncertain change.

RISK MANAGEMENT

To hedge one's risk they will employ financial analysis and trading techniques.

S

SPREAD

The difference between the bid (buy) and offer (ask, sell) prices; in other words the spread is the commission that the brokerage house makes on each trade. This can vary widely between currencies and between brokerage firms. For example, USD/JPY may bid at 131.40 and ask at 131.45, this five-pip spread defines the trader's cost, which can be recovered with a favorable currency move in the market.

STOP LOSS

The ability to manage your losses should a trade reverse its direction.

TRADING TERMS

STOCHASTICS OSCILLATOR

This technical analysis indicator is based on the premise that during an upward trending market, prices tend to close near their high, and during a downward trendiing market, prices tend to close near their low.

SUPPORT LEVELS

A term used in technical analysis indicating a specific price level at which a currency will have the inability to cross below. Recurring failure for the price to move below that point produces a pattern that can usually be shaped by a straight line. It is the opposite of resistance levels.

T

TAKE PROFIT

An order placed to close a position so as to lock profits once it hits a specific price.

TECHNICAL ANALYSIS

An effort to forecast prices by analyzing market action through chart study, volume, trends, moving averages, patterns, formations and many other technical indicators.

TRADING

Buying or selling of goods and services among countries called commerce. Forex Trading is the trading of Foreign Currencies.

TRADING PLAN

A detailed plan on how to trade the financial markets. It is a step-by-step set of instructions on when to enter the market, when to exit with minimal loss once the market goes against you and when to book profits.

TREND

Simply the direction of the market, usually broken down to three categories: major, intermediate and short-term trends.

U

USD

US Dollar. The currency of the United States of America, including these other places: American Samoa, Bonaire, Sint Eustatius and Saba, the British Indian Ocean Territory, Equador, El, Salvador, Guam, Haiti, the Marshall Islands, Federated States of Micronesia, the Northern Mariana Islands, Palau, Panama, Puerto Rico, Timor-Leste, the Turks and Caicos Islands, United States Minor Outlying, British Virgin Islands, U.S. Virgin Islands. It is subdivided into 100 cents.

Y

YIELD

Return on an investment and is usually expressed as a percentage.

COMMONLY TRADED PAIRS

EASTERN STANDARD TIMES

LONDON

3:00 AM-11:00 AM

EUR/USD
AUD/USD
GBP/USD
NZD/USD
USD/JPY
USD/CAD
USD/CHF
GBP/JPY
EUR/JPY
EUR/GBP

NEW YORK

8:00 AM-5:00 PM

EUR/USD
GBP/JPY
GBP/USD
AUD/JPY
AUD/USD
EUR/JPY
USD/CAD
NZD/USD

SYDNEY

3:00 PM-12:00 AM

USD/JPY
EUR/AUD
AUD/JPY
EUR/USD
NZD/USD

TOKYO

7:00 PM-4:00 AM

GBP/JPY
EUR/JPY
AUD/USD
GBP/USD
EUR/USD
USD/CHF

UNDERSTANDING CANDLES

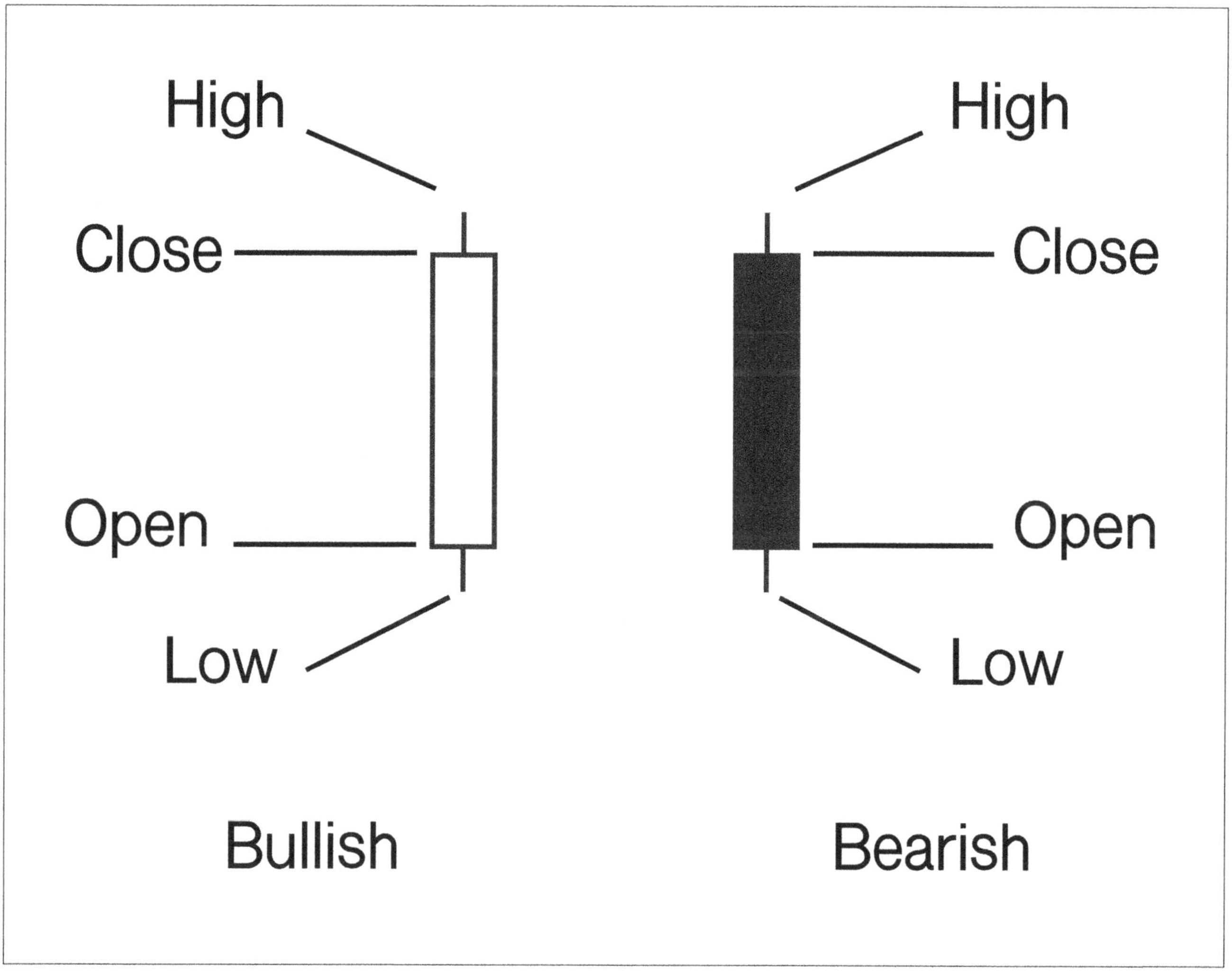

UNDERSTANDING SUPPORT & RESISTANCE

They are areas where the price stops and reverses direction.

Drawing **support** (sometimes called the floor) and **resistance** (sometimes called the ceiling) lines can help you identify market turning points, where to place Take Profits, and Stop Losses.

Once price breaks through support, the support area becomes an area of resistance. Once the price breaks through resistance, the resistance area becomes an area of support.

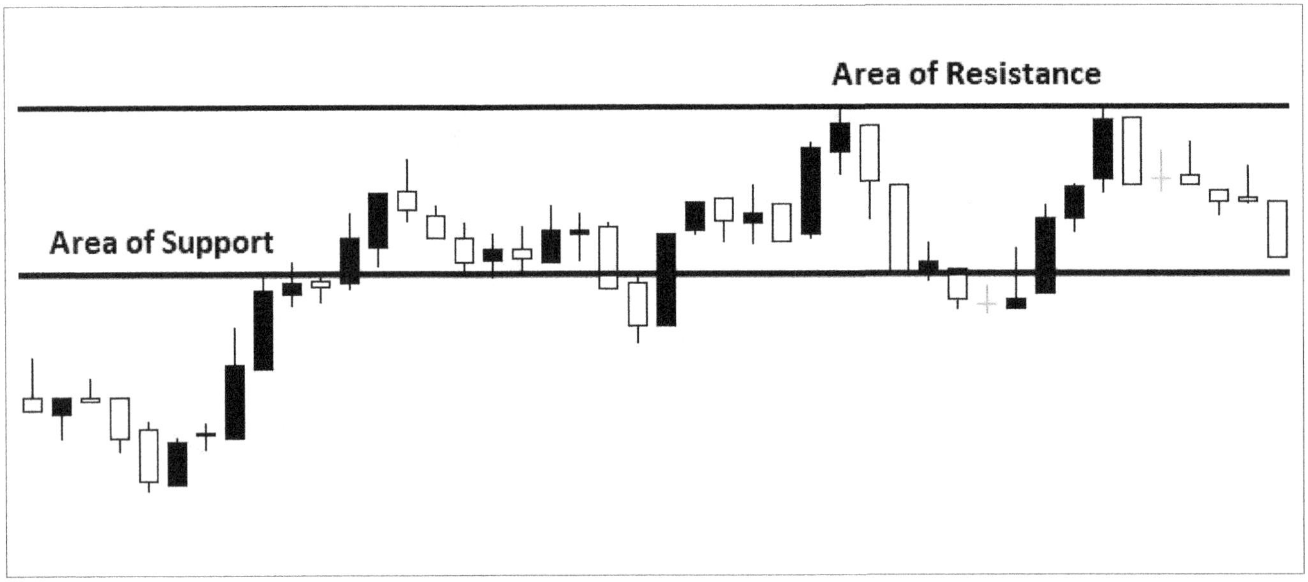

UNDERSTANDING TREND LINES

It is often said that you should trade with the **trend**. What is a **trend**? A **trend** lets you know which direction the market is moving. The market moves in three directions: up, down and sideways. You don't want to be in the market when it is moving sideways.

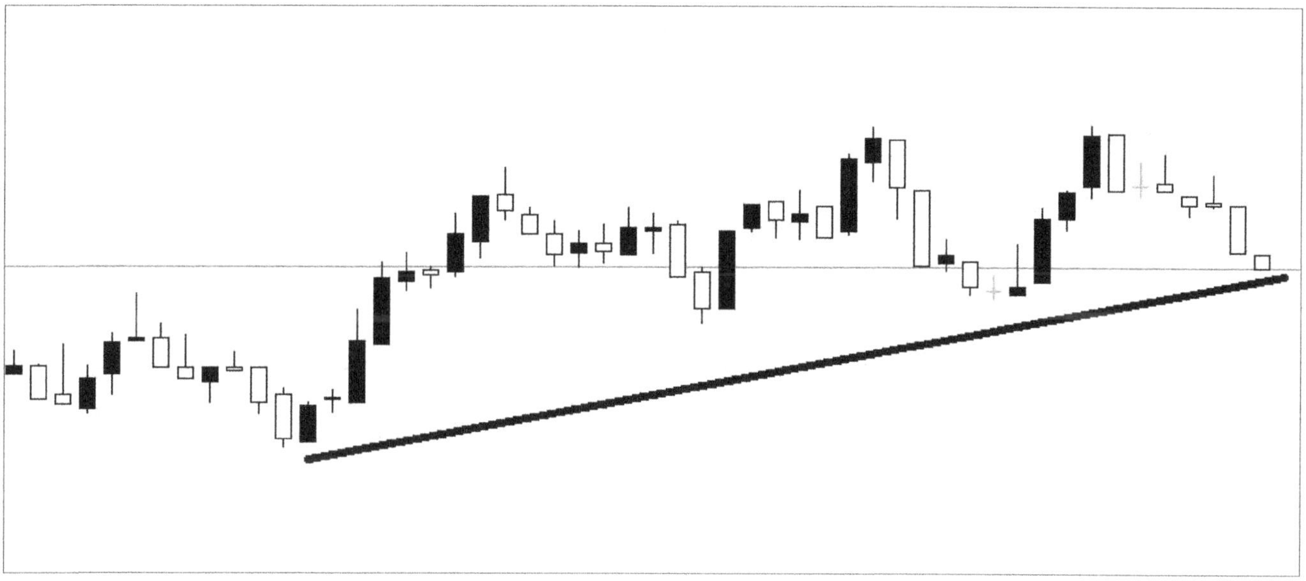

TRADE NUGGETS

1

Let the market come to you.

2

Set a daily financial trading goal.

3

Try to complete at least two trades per day.

4

Remember, the market is impacted by the news.

5

The trend is your friend. Trade with the trend.

THE TRADING PLAN

1

Relax, and be at peace with the market.

2

Practice proper risk management.

3

Never invest more than 50% of your account
in a single trade.

4

Once you've reached your financial goal for the day,
get out of the market.

5

When scalping, remember POPs.
You can Profit Off Pull Backs.

6

Consistency breeds success. Not every trade will end in a win
but we will end the week successfully if we remain consistent.

PIP

TALKS

START HERE

PIP TIPS

It's All About The PIPs

1

PIP: POINTS IN PERCENTAGE

2

LOT SIZE: UNIT OF MEASUREMENT

3

TP: TAKE PROFIT

4

SL: STOP LOSS

PIP COUNTER

MONTH	ACCOUNT SIZE	LOT SIZE	PIPS PER DAY (AVERAGE)	DOLLARS PER PIP	DOLLARS PER PAY	DOLLARS PER MONTH (5 DAYS A WEEK)	DOLLARS PER YEAR
1	1,000.00	.01	10	$1.00	$10.00	$200.00	$2,400.00
2	1,200.00	.02	10	$2.00	$20.00	$400.00	$4,800.00
3	1,600.00	.04	10	$4.00	$40.00	$800.00	$9,600.00
4	2,400.00	.08	10	$8.00	$80.00	$1,600.00	$19,200.00
5	4,000.00	1	10	$10.00	$100.00	$2,000.00	$24,000.00
6	6,000.00	2	10	$20.00	$200.00	$4,000.00	$48,000.00
7	10,000.00	3	10	$30.00	$300.00	$6,000.00	$72,000.00
8	16,000.00	4	10	$40.00	$400.00	$8,000.00	$96,000.00
9	24,000.00	5	10	$50.00	$500.00	$10,000.00	$120,000.00
10	34,000.00	6	10	$60.00	$600.00	$12,000.00	$144,000.00
11	46,000.00	7	10	$70.00	$700.00	$14,000.00	$168,000.00
12	60,000.00	8	10	$80.00	$800.00	$16,000.00	$198,000.00

PROFIT-ABILITY SHEET

To understand the value of a **lot**, you would simply move the decimal point to the right one place to come up with the dollar value. Example: a **lot** size of 1.35 would equal $13.50

MICRO

0.01 = 10 Cents | 0.02 = 20 Cents | 0.03 = 30 Cents | 0.04 = 40 Cents

0.05 = 50 Cents | 0.06 = 60 Cents | 0.07 = 70 Cents | 0.08 = 80 Cents

0.09 = 90 Cents

MINI

0.10 = 1 Dollar | 0.20 = 2 Dollars | 0.30 = 3 Dollars | 0.40 = 4 Dollars

0.50 = 5 Dollars | 0.60 = 60 Dollars | 0.70 = 7 Dollars | 0.80 = 8 Dollars

0.90 = 9 Dollars

STANDARD

1.00 = 10 Dollars | 2.00 = 20 Dollars | 3.00 = 30 Dollars | 4.00 = 40 Dollars

5.00 = 50 Dollars | 6.00 = 60 Dollars | 7.00 = 70 Dollars | 8.00 = 80 Dollars

9.00 = 90 Dollars | 10.00 = 100 Dollars

REPEAT AFTER ME

I will try to do a minimum of 10 PIPs per day

SUCCESS TRADING

STARTS HERE

DON'T FORGET

1. YOUR WEALTH HEALTH ONLY REQUIRES A DECISION
2. WE WIN WHEN WE REFUSE TO LOSE
3. YOU ARE A SUCCESSFUL TRADER
4. STAY TEACHABLE
5. TRADE ACCORDING TO PLAN & PRACTICE PROPER RISK MANAGEMENT

THE GOD OF HEAVEN WILL HELP US TO SUCCEED

NEHEMIAH 2:20

(NEW LIVING TRANSLATION)

DEMO TRADE TRACKER

DATE : ______ BUY ☐ SELL ☐ PAIR : ______

M1 ☐ M5 ☐ M15 ☐ M30 ☐ H1 ☐ H4 ☐ D1 ☐

ENTRY TIME: ______

ENTRY PRICE: ______

LOT SIZE: ______

SPREAD: ______

PIP GOAL: ______

TP/SL

TP1: ______

TP2 : ______

STOP LOSS : ______

PATTERN

☐ ______

☐ ______

TRADE STRATEGY

☐ ______

☐ ______

TRADE RECAP

WIN ☐ LOSS ☐

DEMO TRADE TRACKER

DATE : ____________ BUY ☐ SELL ☐ PAIR : ____________

M1 ☐ M5 ☐ M15 ☐ M30 ☐ H1 ☐ H4 ☐ D1 ☐

ENTRY TIME: ____________

ENTRY PRICE: ____________

LOT SIZE: ____________

SPREAD: ____________

PIP GOAL: ____________

TP/SL

TP1: ____________

TP2 : ____________

STOP LOSS : ____________

PATTERN

☐ ____________

☐ ____________

TRADE STRATEGY

☐ ____________

☐ ____________

TRADE RECAP

WIN ☐ LOSS ☐

DEMO TRADE TRACKER

DATE : ____________ BUY ☐ SELL ☐ PAIR : ____________

M1 ☐ M5 ☐ M15 ☐ M30 ☐ H1 ☐ H4 ☐ D1 ☐

ENTRY TIME: ____________

ENTRY PRICE: ____________

LOT SIZE: ____________

SPREAD: ____________

PIP GOAL: ____________

TRADE RECAP

WIN ☐ LOSS ☐

TP/SL

TP1: ____________

TP2 : ____________

STOP LOSS : ____________

PATTERN

☐ ____________
☐ ____________

TRADE STRATEGY

☐ ____________
☐ ____________

DEMO TRADE TRACKER

DATE : ____________ BUY ☐ SELL ☐ PAIR : ____________

M1 ☐ M5 ☐ M15 ☐ M30 ☐ H1 ☐ H4 ☐ D1 ☐

ENTRY TIME: ____________

ENTRY PRICE: ____________

LOT SIZE: ____________

SPREAD: ____________

PIP GOAL: ____________

TP/SL

TP1: ____________

TP2 : ____________

STOP LOSS : ____________

PATTERN

☐ ____________

☐ ____________

TRADE STRATEGY

☐ ____________

☐ ____________

TRADE RECAP

WIN ☐ LOSS ☐

DEMO TRADE TRACKER

DATE : ______ BUY ☐ SELL ☐ PAIR : ______

M1 ☐ M5 ☐ M15 ☐ M30 ☐ H1 ☐ H4 ☐ D1 ☐

ENTRY TIME: ______

ENTRY PRICE: ______

LOT SIZE: ______

SPREAD: ______

PIP GOAL: ______

TP/SL

TP1: ______

TP2 : ______

STOP LOSS : ______

PATTERN

☐ ______

☐ ______

TRADE RECAP

WIN ☐ LOSS ☐

TRADE STRATEGY

☐ ______

☐ ______

DEMO TRADE TRACKER

DATE : ____________ BUY ☐ SELL ☐ PAIR : ____________

M1 ☐ M5 ☐ M15 ☐ M30 ☐ H1 ☐ H4 ☐ D1 ☐

ENTRY TIME:

ENTRY PRICE:

LOT SIZE:

SPREAD:

PIP GOAL:

TP/SL

TP1:

TP2 :

STOP LOSS :

PATTERN

☐

☐

TRADE RECAP

WIN ☐ LOSS ☐

TRADE STRATEGY

☐

☐

DEMO TRADE TRACKER

DATE : ____________ BUY ☐ SELL ☐ PAIR : ____________

M1 ☐ M5 ☐ M15 ☐ M30 ☐ H1 ☐ H4 ☐ D1 ☐

ENTRY TIME: ____________

ENTRY PRICE: ____________

LOT SIZE: ____________

SPREAD: ____________

PIP GOAL: ____________

TRADE RECAP

WIN ☐ LOSS ☐

TP/SL

TP1: ____________

TP2 : ____________

STOP LOSS : ____________

PATTERN

☐ ____________

☐ ____________

TRADE STRATEGY

☐ ____________

☐ ____________

DEMO TRADE TRACKER

DATE : BUY ☐ SELL ☐ PAIR :

M1 ☐ M5 ☐ M15 ☐ M30 ☐ H1 ☐ H4 ☐ D1 ☐

ENTRY TIME:

ENTRY PRICE:

LOT SIZE:

SPREAD:

PIP GOAL:

TP/SL

TP1:

TP2 :

STOP LOSS :

PATTERN

☐

☐

TRADE RECAP

WIN ☐ LOSS ☐

TRADE STRATEGY

☐

☐

DEMO TRADE TRACKER

DATE : ______ BUY ☐ SELL ☐ PAIR : ______

M1 ☐ M5 ☐ M15 ☐ M30 ☐ H1 ☐ H4 ☐ D1 ☐

ENTRY TIME: ______

ENTRY PRICE: ______

LOT SIZE: ______

SPREAD: ______

PIP GOAL: ______

TP/SL

TP1: ______

TP2 : ______

STOP LOSS : ______

PATTERN

☐ ______
☐ ______

TRADE STRATEGY

☐ ______
☐ ______

TRADE RECAP

WIN ☐ LOSS ☐

DEMO TRADE TRACKER

DATE : ______ BUY ☐ SELL ☐ PAIR : ______

M1 ☐ M5 ☐ M15 ☐ M30 ☐ H1 ☐ H4 ☐ D1 ☐

ENTRY TIME: ______

ENTRY PRICE: ______

LOT SIZE: ______

SPREAD: ______

PIP GOAL: ______

TP/SL

TP1: ______

TP2 : ______

STOP LOSS : ______

PATTERN

☐ ______

☐ ______

TRADE STRATEGY

☐ ______

☐ ______

TRADE RECAP

WIN ☐ LOSS ☐

DEMO REFLECTION (1-10)

VIDEO NOTES

TEAM NOTES

BIGGEST WIN

TEACHABLE MOMENT

NOTES

DEMO TRADE TRACKER

DATE : ____________ BUY ☐ SELL ☐ PAIR : ____________

M1 ☐ M5 ☐ M15 ☐ M30 ☐ H1 ☐ H4 ☐ D1 ☐

ENTRY TIME: ____________

ENTRY PRICE: ____________

LOT SIZE: ____________

SPREAD: ____________

PIP GOAL: ____________

TP/SL

TP1: ____________

TP2 : ____________

STOP LOSS : ____________

PATTERN

☐ ____________

☐ ____________

TRADE STRATEGY

☐ ____________

☐ ____________

TRADE RECAP

WIN ☐ LOSS ☐

DEMO TRADE TRACKER

DATE : ____________ BUY ☐ SELL ☐ PAIR : ____________

M1 ☐ M5 ☐ M15 ☐ M30 ☐ H1 ☐ H4 ☐ D1 ☐

ENTRY TIME: ____________

ENTRY PRICE: ____________

LOT SIZE: ____________

SPREAD: ____________

PIP GOAL: ____________

TP/SL

TP1: ____________

TP2 : ____________

STOP LOSS : ____________

PATTERN

☐ ____________

☐ ____________

TRADE STRATEGY

☐ ____________

☐ ____________

TRADE RECAP

WIN ☐ LOSS ☐

____

____

____

____

____

____

DEMO TRADE TRACKER

DATE : ____________ BUY ☐ SELL ☐ PAIR : ____________

M1 ☐ M5 ☐ M15 ☐ M30 ☐ H1 ☐ H4 ☐ D1 ☐

ENTRY TIME: ____________

ENTRY PRICE: ____________

LOT SIZE: ____________

SPREAD: ____________

PIP GOAL: ____________

TP/SL

TP1: ____________

TP2 : ____________

STOP LOSS : ____________

PATTERN

☐ ____________

☐ ____________

TRADE STRATEGY

☐ ____________

☐ ____________

TRADE RECAP

WIN ☐ LOSS ☐

DEMO TRADE TRACKER

DATE : ____________ BUY ☐ SELL ☐ PAIR : ____________

M1 ☐ M5 ☐ M15 ☐ M30 ☐ H1 ☐ H4 ☐ D1 ☐

ENTRY TIME: ____________

ENTRY PRICE: ____________

LOT SIZE: ____________

SPREAD: ____________

PIP GOAL: ____________

TP/SL

TP1: ____________

TP2 : ____________

STOP LOSS : ____________

PATTERN

☐ ____________

☐ ____________

TRADE RECAP

WIN ☐ LOSS ☐

TRADE STRATEGY

☐ ____________

☐ ____________

DEMO TRADE TRACKER

DATE : ____ BUY ☐ SELL ☐ PAIR : ____

M1 ☐ M5 ☐ M15 ☐ M30 ☐ H1 ☐ H4 ☐ D1 ☐

ENTRY TIME: ____

ENTRY PRICE: ____

LOT SIZE: ____

SPREAD: ____

PIP GOAL: ____

TP/SL

TP1: ____

TP2 : ____

STOP LOSS : ____

PATTERN

☐ ____

☐ ____

TRADE RECAP

WIN ☐ LOSS ☐

TRADE STRATEGY

☐ ____

☐ ____

DEMO TRADE TRACKER

DATE : ____________ BUY ☐ SELL ☐ PAIR : ____________

M1 ☐ M5 ☐ M15 ☐ M30 ☐ H1 ☐ H4 ☐ D1 ☐

ENTRY TIME: ____________

ENTRY PRICE: ____________

LOT SIZE: ____________

SPREAD: ____________

PIP GOAL: ____________

TP/SL

TP1: ____________

TP2 : ____________

STOP LOSS : ____________

PATTERN

☐ ____________

☐ ____________

TRADE STRATEGY

☐ ____________

☐ ____________

TRADE RECAP

WIN ☐ LOSS ☐

DEMO TRADE TRACKER

DATE : ____________ BUY ☐ SELL ☐ PAIR : ____________

M1 ☐ M5 ☐ M15 ☐ M30 ☐ H1 ☐ H4 ☐ D1 ☐

ENTRY TIME: ____________

ENTRY PRICE: ____________

LOT SIZE: ____________

SPREAD: ____________

PIP GOAL: ____________

TP/SL

TP1: ____________

TP2 : ____________

STOP LOSS : ____________

PATTERN

☐ ____________

☐ ____________

TRADE STRATEGY

☐ ____________

☐ ____________

TRADE RECAP

WIN ☐ LOSS ☐

DEMO TRADE TRACKER

DATE : ____________ BUY ☐ SELL ☐ PAIR : ____________

M1 ☐ M5 ☐ M15 ☐ M30 ☐ H1 ☐ H4 ☐ D1 ☐

ENTRY TIME: ____________

ENTRY PRICE: ____________

LOT SIZE: ____________

SPREAD: ____________

PIP GOAL: ____________

TP/SL

TP1: ____________

TP2 : ____________

STOP LOSS : ____________

PATTERN

☐ ____________

☐ ____________

TRADE STRATEGY

☐ ____________

☐ ____________

TRADE RECAP

WIN ☐ LOSS ☐

DEMO TRADE TRACKER

DATE : ____________ BUY ☐ SELL ☐ PAIR : ____________

M1 ☐ M5 ☐ M15 ☐ M30 ☐ H1 ☐ H4 ☐ D1 ☐

ENTRY TIME: ____________

ENTRY PRICE: ____________

LOT SIZE: ____________

SPREAD: ____________

PIP GOAL: ____________

TP/SL

TP1: ____________

TP2 : ____________

STOP LOSS : ____________

PATTERN

☐ ____________

☐ ____________

TRADE RECAP

WIN ☐ LOSS ☐

TRADE STRATEGY

☐ ____________

☐ ____________

DEMO TRADE TRACKER

DATE : ____________ BUY ☐ SELL ☐ PAIR : ____________

M1 ☐ M5 ☐ M15 ☐ M30 ☐ H1 ☐ H4 ☐ D1 ☐

ENTRY TIME: ____________

ENTRY PRICE: ____________

LOT SIZE: ____________

SPREAD: ____________

PIP GOAL: ____________

TP/SL

TP1: ____________

TP2 : ____________

STOP LOSS : ____________

PATTERN

☐ ____________

☐ ____________

TRADE STRATEGY

☐ ____________

☐ ____________

TRADE RECAP

WIN ☐ LOSS ☐

DEMO REFLECTION (11-20)

VIDEO NOTES

TEAM NOTES

BIGGEST WIN

TEACHABLE MOMENT

NOTES

MAKE IT

A

BLUE-

TIFUL

DAY

LIVE TRADES

START HERE

JUST REMEMBER

1

DON'T LEVERAGE MORE THAN
3% OF YOUR ACCOUNT

2

BE FAITHFUL TO
THE SKILL-SET

3

IF TP IS **ABOVE** THE ENTRY
POINT, IT'S A BUY

IF TP IS **BELOW** THE ENTRY
POINT, IT'S A SELL

4

WINS ATTRACT WEALTH

LIVE TRADE TRACKER

DATE : ____________ BUY ☐ SELL ☐ PAIR : ____________

M1 ☐ M5 ☐ M15 ☐ M30 ☐ H1 ☐ H4 ☐ D1 ☐

ENTRY TIME:

ENTRY PRICE:

LOT SIZE:

SPREAD:

PIP GOAL:

TRADE RECAP

WIN ☐ LOSS ☐

TP/SL

TP1:

TP2 :

STOP LOSS :

PATTERN

☐

☐

TRADE STRATEGY

☐

☐

LIVE TRADE TRACKER

DATE : ____________ BUY ☐ SELL ☐ PAIR : ____________

M1 ☐ M5 ☐ M15 ☐ M30 ☐ H1 ☐ H4 ☐ D1 ☐

ENTRY
TIME:

ENTRY
PRICE:

LOT SIZE:

SPREAD:

PIP GOAL:

TP/SL

TP1:

TP2 :

STOP LOSS :

PATTERN

☐
☐

TRADE STRATEGY

☐
☐

TRADE RECAP

WIN ☐ LOSS ☐

LIVE TRADE TRACKER

DATE : ____________ BUY ☐ SELL ☐ PAIR : ____________

M1 ☐ M5 ☐ M15 ☐ M30 ☐ H1 ☐ H4 ☐ D1 ☐

ENTRY TIME: ____________

ENTRY PRICE: ____________

LOT SIZE: ____________

SPREAD: ____________

PIP GOAL: ____________

TP/SL

TP1: ____________

TP2 : ____________

STOP LOSS : ____________

PATTERN

☐ ____________

☐ ____________

TRADE STRATEGY

☐ ____________

☐ ____________

TRADE RECAP

WIN ☐ LOSS ☐

LIVE TRADE TRACKER

DATE : ______ BUY ☐ SELL ☐ PAIR : ______

M1 ☐ M5 ☐ M15 ☐ M30 ☐ H1 ☐ H4 ☐ D1 ☐

ENTRY TIME:

ENTRY PRICE:

LOT SIZE:

SPREAD:

PIP GOAL:

TP/SL

TP1:

TP2 :

STOP LOSS :

PATTERN

☐

☐

TRADE RECAP

WIN ☐ LOSS ☐

TRADE STRATEGY

☐

☐

LIVE TRADE TRACKER

DATE : ____________ BUY ☐ SELL ☐ PAIR : ____________

M1 ☐ M5 ☐ M15 ☐ M30 ☐ H1 ☐ H4 ☐ D1 ☐

ENTRY TIME: ____________

ENTRY PRICE: ____________

LOT SIZE: ____________

SPREAD: ____________

PIP GOAL: ____________

TP/SL

TP1: ____________

TP2 : ____________

STOP LOSS : ____________

PATTERN

☐ ____________

☐ ____________

TRADE STRATEGY

☐ ____________

☐ ____________

TRADE RECAP

WIN ☐ LOSS ☐

LIVE TRADE TRACKER

DATE : ____________ BUY ☐ SELL ☐ PAIR : ____________

M1 ☐ M5 ☐ M15 ☐ M30 ☐ H1 ☐ H4 ☐ D1 ☐

ENTRY TIME:

ENTRY PRICE:

LOT SIZE:

SPREAD:

PIP GOAL:

TRADE RECAP

WIN ☐ LOSS ☐

TP/SL

TP1:

TP2 :

STOP LOSS :

PATTERN

☐ ____________

☐ ____________

TRADE STRATEGY

☐ ____________

☐ ____________

LIVE TRADE TRACKER

DATE : ____________ BUY ☐ SELL ☐ PAIR : ____________

M1 ☐ M5 ☐ M15 ☐ M30 ☐ H1 ☐ H4 ☐ D1 ☐

ENTRY
TIME: ____________

ENTRY
PRICE: ____________

LOT SIZE: ____________

SPREAD: ____________

PIP GOAL: ____________

TP/SL

TP1: ____________

TP2 : ____________

STOP LOSS : ____________

PATTERN

☐ ____________

☐ ____________

TRADE RECAP

WIN ☐ LOSS ☐

TRADE STRATEGY

☐ ____________

☐ ____________

LIVE TRADE TRACKER

DATE : ______ BUY ☐ SELL ☐ PAIR : ______

M1 ☐ M5 ☐ M15 ☐ M30 ☐ H1 ☐ H4 ☐ D1 ☐

ENTRY TIME: ______

ENTRY PRICE: ______

LOT SIZE: ______

SPREAD: ______

PIP GOAL: ______

TP/SL

TP1: ______

TP2 : ______

STOP LOSS : ______

PATTERN

☐ ______

☐ ______

TRADE RECAP

WIN ☐ LOSS ☐

TRADE STRATEGY

☐ ______

☐ ______

LIVE TRADE TRACKER

DATE : ____________ BUY ☐ SELL ☐ PAIR : ____________

M1 ☐ M5 ☐ M15 ☐ M30 ☐ H1 ☐ H4 ☐ D1 ☐

ENTRY TIME: ____________

ENTRY PRICE: ____________

LOT SIZE: ____________

SPREAD: ____________

PIP GOAL: ____________

TP/SL

TP1: ____________

TP2 : ____________

STOP LOSS : ____________

PATTERN

☐ ____________

☐ ____________

TRADE RECAP

WIN ☐ LOSS ☐

TRADE STRATEGY

☐ ____________

☐ ____________

LIVE TRADE TRACKER

DATE : ______ BUY ☐ SELL ☐ PAIR : ______

M1 ☐ M5 ☐ M15 ☐ M30 ☐ H1 ☐ H4 ☐ D1 ☐

ENTRY TIME: ______

ENTRY PRICE: ______

LOT SIZE: ______

SPREAD: ______

PIP GOAL: ______

TP/SL

TP1: ______

TP2 : ______

STOP LOSS : ______

PATTERN

☐ ______

☐ ______

TRADE RECAP

WIN ☐ LOSS ☐

TRADE STRATEGY

☐ ______

☐ ______

LIVE REFLECTION (1-10)

VIDEO NOTES

TEAM NOTES

BIGGEST WIN

TEACHABLE MOMENT

NOTES

LIVE TRADE TRACKER

DATE : ____________ BUY ☐ SELL ☐ PAIR : ____________

M1 ☐ M5 ☐ M15 ☐ M30 ☐ H1 ☐ H4 ☐ D1 ☐

ENTRY TIME: ____________

ENTRY PRICE: ____________

LOT SIZE: ____________

SPREAD: ____________

PIP GOAL: ____________

TP/SL

TP1: ____________

TP2 : ____________

STOP LOSS : ____________

PATTERN

☐ ____________

☐ ____________

TRADE RECAP

WIN ☐ LOSS ☐

TRADE STRATEGY

☐ ____________

☐ ____________

LIVE TRADE TRACKER

DATE : ____________ BUY ☐ SELL ☐ PAIR : ____________

M1 ☐ M5 ☐ M15 ☐ M30 ☐ H1 ☐ H4 ☐ D1 ☐

ENTRY TIME: ____________

ENTRY PRICE: ____________

LOT SIZE: ____________

SPREAD: ____________

PIP GOAL: ____________

TP/SL

TP1: ____________

TP2 : ____________

STOP LOSS : ____________

PATTERN

☐ ____________

☐ ____________

TRADE STRATEGY

☐ ____________

☐ ____________

TRADE RECAP

WIN ☐ LOSS ☐

LIVE TRADE TRACKER

DATE : ____________ BUY ☐ SELL ☐ PAIR : ____________

M1 ☐ M5 ☐ M15 ☐ M30 ☐ H1 ☐ H4 ☐ D1 ☐

ENTRY TIME: ____________

ENTRY PRICE: ____________

LOT SIZE: ____________

SPREAD: ____________

PIP GOAL: ____________

TP/SL

TP1: ____________

TP2 : ____________

STOP LOSS : ____________

PATTERN

☐ ____________

☐ ____________

TRADE STRATEGY

☐ ____________

☐ ____________

TRADE RECAP

WIN ☐ LOSS ☐

LIVE TRADE TRACKER

DATE : ____________ BUY ☐ SELL ☐ PAIR : ____________

M1 ☐ M5 ☐ M15 ☐ M30 ☐ H1 ☐ H4 ☐ D1 ☐

ENTRY TIME: ____________

ENTRY PRICE: ____________

LOT SIZE: ____________

SPREAD: ____________

PIP GOAL: ____________

TRADE RECAP

WIN ☐ LOSS ☐

TP/SL

TP1: ____________

TP2 : ____________

STOP LOSS : ____________

PATTERN

☐ ____________

☐ ____________

TRADE STRATEGY

☐ ____________

☐ ____________

LIVE TRADE TRACKER

DATE : ____________ BUY ☐ SELL ☐ PAIR : ____________

M1 ☐ M5 ☐ M15 ☐ M30 ☐ H1 ☐ H4 ☐ D1 ☐

ENTRY TIME: ____________

ENTRY PRICE: ____________

LOT SIZE: ____________

SPREAD: ____________

PIP GOAL: ____________

TP/SL

TP1: ____________

TP2 : ____________

STOP LOSS : ____________

PATTERN

☐ ____________
☐ ____________

TRADE RECAP

WIN ☐ LOSS ☐

TRADE STRATEGY

☐ ____________
☐ ____________

LIVE TRADE TRACKER

DATE : ______ BUY ☐ SELL ☐ PAIR : ______

M1 ☐ M5 ☐ M15 ☐ M30 ☐ H1 ☐ H4 ☐ D1 ☐

ENTRY TIME: ______

ENTRY PRICE: ______

LOT SIZE: ______

SPREAD: ______

PIP GOAL: ______

TP/SL

TP1: ______

TP2 : ______

STOP LOSS : ______

PATTERN

☐ ______

☐ ______

TRADE RECAP

WIN ☐ LOSS ☐

TRADE STRATEGY

☐ ______

☐ ______

LIVE TRADE TRACKER

DATE : ____________ BUY ☐ SELL ☐ PAIR : ____________

M1 ☐ M5 ☐ M15 ☐ M30 ☐ H1 ☐ H4 ☐ D1 ☐

TP/SL

TP1: ____________

TP2 : ____________

STOP LOSS : ____________

ENTRY TIME: ____________

ENTRY PRICE: ____________

LOT SIZE: ____________

PATTERN

☐ ____________

☐ ____________

SPREAD: ____________

PIP GOAL: ____________

TRADE RECAP

WIN ☐ LOSS ☐

TRADE STRATEGY

☐ ____________

☐ ____________

LIVE TRADE TRACKER

DATE : ____________ BUY ☐ SELL ☐ PAIR : ____________

M1 ☐ M5 ☐ M15 ☐ M30 ☐ H1 ☐ H4 ☐ D1 ☐

ENTRY TIME: ____________

ENTRY PRICE: ____________

LOT SIZE: ____________

SPREAD: ____________

PIP GOAL: ____________

TP/SL

TP1: ____________

TP2 : ____________

STOP LOSS : ____________

PATTERN

☐ ____________

☐ ____________

TRADE RECAP

WIN ☐ LOSS ☐

TRADE STRATEGY

☐ ____________

☐ ____________

LIVE TRADE TRACKER

DATE : ______ BUY ☐ SELL ☐ PAIR : ______

M1 ☐ M5 ☐ M15 ☐ M30 ☐ H1 ☐ H4 ☐ D1 ☐

ENTRY TIME: ______

ENTRY PRICE: ______

LOT SIZE: ______

SPREAD: ______

PIP GOAL: ______

TP/SL

TP1: ______

TP2 : ______

STOP LOSS : ______

PATTERN

☐ ______

☐ ______

TRADE STRATEGY

☐ ______

☐ ______

TRADE RECAP

WIN ☐ LOSS ☐

LIVE TRADE TRACKER

DATE : ________ BUY ☐ SELL ☐ PAIR : ________

M1 ☐ M5 ☐ M15 ☐ M30 ☐ H1 ☐ H4 ☐ D1 ☐

ENTRY TIME: ________

ENTRY PRICE: ________

LOT SIZE: ________

SPREAD: ________

PIP GOAL: ________

TP/SL

TP1: ________

TP2 : ________

STOP LOSS : ________

PATTERN

☐ ________

☐ ________

TRADE RECAP

WIN ☐ LOSS ☐

TRADE STRATEGY

☐ ________

☐ ________

LIVE REFLECTION (11-20)

VIDEO NOTES

TEAM NOTES

BIGGEST WIN

TEACHABLE MOMENT

NOTES

LIVE TRADE TRACKER

DATE : ______ BUY ☐ SELL ☐ PAIR : ______

M1 ☐ M5 ☐ M15 ☐ M30 ☐ H1 ☐ H4 ☐ D1 ☐

ENTRY TIME: ______

ENTRY PRICE: ______

LOT SIZE: ______

SPREAD: ______

PIP GOAL: ______

TRADE RECAP

WIN ☐ LOSS ☐

TP/SL

TP1: ______

TP2 : ______

STOP LOSS : ______

PATTERN

☐ ______

☐ ______

TRADE STRATEGY

☐ ______

☐ ______

LIVE TRADE TRACKER

DATE : ____________ BUY ☐ SELL ☐ PAIR : ____________

M1 ☐ M5 ☐ M15 ☐ M30 ☐ H1 ☐ H4 ☐ D1 ☐

ENTRY TIME: ____________

ENTRY PRICE: ____________

LOT SIZE: ____________

SPREAD: ____________

PIP GOAL: ____________

TP/SL

TP1: ____________

TP2 : ____________

STOP LOSS : ____________

PATTERN

☐ ____________

☐ ____________

TRADE RECAP

WIN ☐ LOSS ☐

TRADE STRATEGY

☐ ____________

☐ ____________

LIVE TRADE TRACKER

DATE : ____________ BUY ☐ SELL ☐ PAIR : ____________

M1 ☐ M5 ☐ M15 ☐ M30 ☐ H1 ☐ H4 ☐ D1 ☐

ENTRY TIME:

ENTRY PRICE:

LOT SIZE:

SPREAD:

PIP GOAL:

TP/SL

TP1:

TP2 :

STOP LOSS :

PATTERN

☐

☐

TRADE RECAP

WIN ☐ LOSS ☐

TRADE STRATEGY

☐

☐

LIVE TRADE TRACKER

DATE : ____________ BUY ☐ SELL ☐ PAIR : ____________

M1 ☐ M5 ☐ M15 ☐ M30 ☐ H1 ☐ H4 ☐ D1 ☐

ENTRY TIME: ____________

ENTRY PRICE: ____________

LOT SIZE: ____________

SPREAD: ____________

PIP GOAL: ____________

TP/SL

TP1: ____________

TP2 : ____________

STOP LOSS : ____________

PATTERN

☐ ____________

☐ ____________

TRADE STRATEGY

☐ ____________

☐ ____________

TRADE RECAP

WIN ☐ LOSS ☐

LIVE TRADE TRACKER

DATE : ______ BUY ☐ SELL ☐ PAIR : ______

M1 ☐ M5 ☐ M15 ☐ M30 ☐ H1 ☐ H4 ☐ D1 ☐

ENTRY TIME: ______

ENTRY PRICE: ______

LOT SIZE: ______

SPREAD: ______

PIP GOAL: ______

TP/SL

TP1: ______

TP2 : ______

STOP LOSS : ______

PATTERN

☐ ______

☐ ______

TRADE RECAP

WIN ☐ LOSS ☐

TRADE STRATEGY

☐ ______

☐ ______

LIVE TRADE TRACKER

DATE : ____________ BUY ☐ SELL ☐ PAIR : ____________

M1 ☐ M5 ☐ M15 ☐ M30 ☐ H1 ☐ H4 ☐ D1 ☐

ENTRY TIME:

ENTRY PRICE:

LOT SIZE:

SPREAD:

PIP GOAL:

TP/SL

TP1:

TP2 :

STOP LOSS :

PATTERN

☐
☐

TRADE RECAP

WIN ☐ LOSS ☐

TRADE STRATEGY

☐
☐

LIVE TRADE TRACKER

DATE : ____________ BUY ☐ SELL ☐ PAIR : ____________

M1 ☐ M5 ☐ M15 ☐ M30 ☐ H1 ☐ H4 ☐ D1 ☐

ENTRY TIME: ____________

ENTRY PRICE: ____________

LOT SIZE: ____________

SPREAD: ____________

PIP GOAL: ____________

TP/SL

TP1: ____________

TP2 : ____________

STOP LOSS : ____________

PATTERN

☐ ____________

☐ ____________

TRADE RECAP

WIN ☐ LOSS ☐

TRADE STRATEGY

☐ ____________

☐ ____________

LIVE TRADE TRACKER

DATE : ______ BUY ☐ SELL ☐ PAIR : ______

M1 ☐ M5 ☐ M15 ☐ M30 ☐ H1 ☐ H4 ☐ D1 ☐

ENTRY TIME: ______

ENTRY PRICE: ______

LOT SIZE: ______

SPREAD: ______

PIP GOAL: ______

TP/SL

TP1: ______

TP2 : ______

STOP LOSS : ______

PATTERN

☐ ______

☐ ______

TRADE STRATEGY

☐ ______

☐ ______

TRADE RECAP

WIN ☐ LOSS ☐

LIVE TRADE TRACKER

DATE : ______ BUY ☐ SELL ☐ PAIR : ______

M1 ☐ M5 ☐ M15 ☐ M30 ☐ H1 ☐ H4 ☐ D1 ☐

ENTRY TIME: ______

ENTRY PRICE: ______

LOT SIZE: ______

SPREAD: ______

PIP GOAL: ______

TP/SL

TP1: ______

TP2 : ______

STOP LOSS : ______

PATTERN

☐ ______

☐ ______

TRADE STRATEGY

☐ ______

☐ ______

TRADE RECAP

WIN ☐ LOSS ☐

LIVE TRADE TRACKER

DATE : ____________ BUY ☐ SELL ☐ PAIR : ____________

M1 ☐ M5 ☐ M15 ☐ M30 ☐ H1 ☐ H4 ☐ D1 ☐

ENTRY TIME: ____________

ENTRY PRICE: ____________

LOT SIZE: ____________

SPREAD: ____________

PIP GOAL: ____________

TP/SL

TP1: ____________

TP2 : ____________

STOP LOSS : ____________

PATTERN

☐ ____________

☐ ____________

TRADE STRATEGY

☐ ____________

☐ ____________

TRADE RECAP

WIN ☐ LOSS ☐

LIVE REFLECTION (21-30)

VIDEO NOTES

TEAM NOTES

BIGGEST WIN

TEACHABLE MOMENT

NOTES

LIVE TRADE TRACKER

DATE : ____________ BUY ☐ SELL ☐ PAIR : ____________

M1 ☐ M5 ☐ M15 ☐ M30 ☐ H1 ☐ H4 ☐ D1 ☐

ENTRY TIME: ____________

ENTRY PRICE: ____________

LOT SIZE: ____________

SPREAD: ____________

PIP GOAL: ____________

TP/SL

TP1: ____________

TP2 : ____________

STOP LOSS : ____________

PATTERN

☐ ____________

☐ ____________

TRADE RECAP

WIN ☐ LOSS ☐

TRADE STRATEGY

☐ ____________

☐ ____________

LIVE TRADE TRACKER

DATE : ____________ BUY ☐ SELL ☐ PAIR : ____________

M1 ☐ M5 ☐ M15 ☐ M30 ☐ H1 ☐ H4 ☐ D1 ☐

ENTRY TIME: ____________

ENTRY PRICE: ____________

LOT SIZE: ____________

SPREAD: ____________

PIP GOAL: ____________

TP/SL

TP1: ____________

TP2 : ____________

STOP LOSS : ____________

PATTERN

☐ ____________

☐ ____________

TRADE STRATEGY

☐ ____________

☐ ____________

TRADE RECAP

WIN ☐ LOSS ☐

LIVE TRADE TRACKER

DATE : ____________ BUY ☐ SELL ☐ PAIR : ____________

M1 ☐ M5 ☐ M15 ☐ M30 ☐ H1 ☐ H4 ☐ D1 ☐

TP/SL

TP1: ____________

TP2 : ____________

STOP LOSS : ____________

ENTRY TIME: ____________

ENTRY PRICE: ____________

LOT SIZE: ____________

PATTERN

☐ ____________

☐ ____________

SPREAD: ____________

PIP GOAL: ____________

TRADE RECAP

WIN ☐ LOSS ☐

TRADE STRATEGY

☐ ____________

☐ ____________

LIVE TRADE TRACKER

DATE : ____________ BUY ☐ SELL ☐ PAIR : ____________

M1 ☐ M5 ☐ M15 ☐ M30 ☐ H1 ☐ H4 ☐ D1 ☐

ENTRY TIME: ____________

ENTRY PRICE: ____________

LOT SIZE: ____________

SPREAD: ____________

PIP GOAL: ____________

TP/SL

TP1: ____________

TP2 : ____________

STOP LOSS : ____________

PATTERN

☐ ____________

☐ ____________

TRADE STRATEGY

☐ ____________

☐ ____________

TRADE RECAP

WIN ☐ LOSS ☐

LIVE TRADE TRACKER

DATE : ____ BUY ☐ SELL ☐ PAIR : ____

M1 ☐ M5 ☐ M15 ☐ M30 ☐ H1 ☐ H4 ☐ D1 ☐

ENTRY TIME: ____

ENTRY PRICE: ____

LOT SIZE: ____

SPREAD: ____

PIP GOAL: ____

TP/SL

TP1: ____

TP2 : ____

STOP LOSS : ____

PATTERN

☐ ____

☐ ____

TRADE STRATEGY

☐ ____

☐ ____

TRADE RECAP

WIN ☐ LOSS ☐

LIVE TRADE TRACKER

DATE : ________ BUY ☐ SELL ☐ PAIR : ________

M1 ☐ M5 ☐ M15 ☐ M30 ☐ H1 ☐ H4 ☐ D1 ☐

ENTRY TIME:

ENTRY PRICE:

LOT SIZE:

SPREAD:

PIP GOAL:

TP/SL

TP1:

TP2 :

STOP LOSS :

PATTERN

☐

☐

TRADE RECAP

WIN ☐ LOSS ☐

TRADE STRATEGY

☐

☐

LIVE TRADE TRACKER

DATE : ____________ BUY ☐ SELL ☐ PAIR : ____________

M1 ☐ M5 ☐ M15 ☐ M30 ☐ H1 ☐ H4 ☐ D1 ☐

ENTRY TIME: ____________

ENTRY PRICE: ____________

LOT SIZE: ____________

SPREAD: ____________

PIP GOAL: ____________

TP/SL

TP1: ____________

TP2 : ____________

STOP LOSS : ____________

PATTERN

☐ ____________

☐ ____________

TRADE STRATEGY

☐ ____________

☐ ____________

TRADE RECAP

WIN ☐ LOSS ☐

LIVE TRADE TRACKER

DATE : ______ BUY ☐ SELL ☐ PAIR : ______

M1 ☐ M5 ☐ M15 ☐ M30 ☐ H1 ☐ H4 ☐ D1 ☐

ENTRY TIME: ______

ENTRY PRICE: ______

LOT SIZE: ______

SPREAD: ______

PIP GOAL: ______

TP/SL

TP1: ______

TP2 : ______

STOP LOSS : ______

PATTERN

☐ ______

☐ ______

TRADE STRATEGY

☐ ______

☐ ______

TRADE RECAP

WIN ☐ LOSS ☐

LIVE TRADE TRACKER

DATE : ____________ BUY ☐ SELL ☐ PAIR : ____________

M1 ☐ M5 ☐ M15 ☐ M30 ☐ H1 ☐ H4 ☐ D1 ☐

ENTRY TIME: ____________

ENTRY PRICE: ____________

LOT SIZE: ____________

SPREAD: ____________

PIP GOAL: ____________

TP/SL

TP1: ____________

TP2 : ____________

STOP LOSS : ____________

PATTERN

☐ ____________

☐ ____________

TRADE STRATEGY

☐ ____________

☐ ____________

TRADE RECAP

WIN ☐ LOSS ☐

LIVE TRADE TRACKER

DATE : ____________ BUY ☐ SELL ☐ PAIR : ____________

M1 ☐ M5 ☐ M15 ☐ M30 ☐ H1 ☐ H4 ☐ D1 ☐

ENTRY TIME: ____________

ENTRY PRICE: ____________

LOT SIZE: ____________

SPREAD: ____________

PIP GOAL: ____________

TP/SL

TP1: ____________

TP2 : ____________

STOP LOSS : ____________

PATTERN

☐ ____________

☐ ____________

TRADE STRATEGY

☐ ____________

☐ ____________

TRADE RECAP

WIN ☐ LOSS ☐

LIVE REFLECTION (31-40)

VIDEO NOTES

TEAM NOTES

BIGGEST WIN

TEACHABLE MOMENT

NOTES

LIVE TRADE TRACKER

DATE : ______ BUY ☐ SELL ☐ PAIR : ______

M1 ☐ M5 ☐ M15 ☐ M30 ☐ H1 ☐ H4 ☐ D1 ☐

ENTRY TIME:

ENTRY PRICE:

LOT SIZE:

SPREAD:

PIP GOAL:

TP/SL

TP1:

TP2 :

STOP LOSS :

PATTERN

☐

☐

TRADE STRATEGY

☐

☐

TRADE RECAP

WIN ☐ LOSS ☐

LIVE TRADE TRACKER

DATE : ____________ BUY ☐ SELL ☐ PAIR : ____________

M1 ☐ M5 ☐ M15 ☐ M30 ☐ H1 ☐ H4 ☐ D1 ☐

ENTRY TIME: ____________

ENTRY PRICE: ____________

LOT SIZE: ____________

SPREAD: ____________

PIP GOAL: ____________

TP/SL

TP1: ____________

TP2 : ____________

STOP LOSS : ____________

PATTERN

☐ ____________

☐ ____________

TRADE STRATEGY

☐ ____________

☐ ____________

TRADE RECAP

WIN ☐ LOSS ☐

LIVE TRADE TRACKER

DATE : ______ BUY ☐ SELL ☐ PAIR : ______

M1 ☐ M5 ☐ M15 ☐ M30 ☐ H1 ☐ H4 ☐ D1 ☐

ENTRY TIME: ______

ENTRY PRICE: ______

LOT SIZE: ______

SPREAD: ______

PIP GOAL: ______

TP/SL

TP1: ______

TP2 : ______

STOP LOSS : ______

PATTERN

☐ ______

☐ ______

TRADE STRATEGY

☐ ______

☐ ______

TRADE RECAP

WIN ☐ LOSS ☐

LIVE TRADE TRACKER

DATE : ____________ BUY ☐ SELL ☐ PAIR : ____________

M1 ☐ M5 ☐ M15 ☐ M30 ☐ H1 ☐ H4 ☐ D1 ☐

ENTRY TIME: ____________

ENTRY PRICE: ____________

LOT SIZE: ____________

SPREAD: ____________

PIP GOAL: ____________

TP/SL

TP1: ____________

TP2 : ____________

STOP LOSS : ____________

PATTERN

☐ ____________

☐ ____________

TRADE RECAP

WIN ☐ LOSS ☐

TRADE STRATEGY

☐ ____________

☐ ____________

LIVE TRADE TRACKER

DATE : ______ BUY ☐ SELL ☐ PAIR : ______

M1 ☐ M5 ☐ M15 ☐ M30 ☐ H1 ☐ H4 ☐ D1 ☐

ENTRY TIME:

ENTRY PRICE:

LOT SIZE:

SPREAD:

PIP GOAL:

TP/SL

TP1:

TP2 :

STOP LOSS :

PATTERN

☐

☐

TRADE STRATEGY

☐

☐

TRADE RECAP

WIN ☐ LOSS ☐

LIVE TRADE TRACKER

DATE : ____________ BUY ☐ SELL ☐ PAIR : ____________

M1 ☐ M5 ☐ M15 ☐ M30 ☐ H1 ☐ H4 ☐ D1 ☐

ENTRY TIME: ____________

ENTRY PRICE: ____________

LOT SIZE: ____________

SPREAD: ____________

PIP GOAL: ____________

TP/SL

TP1: ____________

TP2 : ____________

STOP LOSS : ____________

PATTERN

☐ ____________

☐ ____________

TRADE STRATEGY

☐ ____________

☐ ____________

TRADE RECAP

WIN ☐ LOSS ☐

LIVE TRADE TRACKER

DATE : ____________ BUY ☐ SELL ☐ PAIR : ____________

M1 ☐ M5 ☐ M15 ☐ M30 ☐ H1 ☐ H4 ☐ D1 ☐

ENTRY TIME: ____________

ENTRY PRICE: ____________

LOT SIZE: ____________

SPREAD: ____________

PIP GOAL: ____________

TP/SL

TP1: ____________

TP2 : ____________

STOP LOSS : ____________

PATTERN

☐ ____________

☐ ____________

TRADE STRATEGY

☐ ____________

☐ ____________

TRADE RECAP

WIN ☐ LOSS ☐

LIVE TRADE TRACKER

DATE : ____________ BUY ☐ SELL ☐ PAIR : ____________

M1 ☐ M5 ☐ M15 ☐ M30 ☐ H1 ☐ H4 ☐ D1 ☐

ENTRY TIME: ____________

ENTRY PRICE: ____________

LOT SIZE: ____________

SPREAD: ____________

PIP GOAL: ____________

TP/SL

TP1: ____________

TP2 : ____________

STOP LOSS : ____________

PATTERN

☐ ____________

☐ ____________

TRADE STRATEGY

☐ ____________

☐ ____________

TRADE RECAP

WIN ☐ LOSS ☐

LIVE TRADE TRACKER

DATE : ____________ BUY ☐ SELL ☐ PAIR : ____________

M1 ☐ M5 ☐ M15 ☐ M30 ☐ H1 ☐ H4 ☐ D1 ☐

ENTRY TIME: ____________

ENTRY PRICE: ____________

LOT SIZE: ____________

SPREAD: ____________

PIP GOAL: ____________

TP/SL

TP1: ____________

TP2 : ____________

STOP LOSS : ____________

PATTERN

☐ ____________

☐ ____________

TRADE STRATEGY

☐ ____________

☐ ____________

TRADE RECAP

WIN ☐ LOSS ☐

LIVE TRADE TRACKER

DATE : ______ BUY ☐ SELL ☐ PAIR : ______

M1 ☐ M5 ☐ M15 ☐ M30 ☐ H1 ☐ H4 ☐ D1 ☐

ENTRY TIME: ______

ENTRY PRICE: ______

LOT SIZE: ______

SPREAD: ______

PIP GOAL: ______

TP/SL

TP1: ______

TP2 : ______

STOP LOSS : ______

PATTERN

☐ ______

☐ ______

TRADE STRATEGY

☐ ______

☐ ______

TRADE RECAP

WIN ☐ LOSS ☐

LIVE REFLECTION (41-50)

VIDEO NOTES

TEAM NOTES

BIGGEST WIN

TEACHABLE MOMENT

NOTES

LIVE TRADE TRACKER

DATE : ______ BUY ☐ SELL ☐ PAIR : ______

M1 ☐ M5 ☐ M15 ☐ M30 ☐ H1 ☐ H4 ☐ D1 ☐

ENTRY TIME: ______

ENTRY PRICE: ______

LOT SIZE: ______

SPREAD: ______

PIP GOAL: ______

TP/SL

TP1: ______

TP2 : ______

STOP LOSS : ______

PATTERN

☐ ______

☐ ______

TRADE RECAP

WIN ☐ LOSS ☐

TRADE STRATEGY

☐ ______

☐ ______

LIVE TRADE TRACKER

DATE : ____________ BUY ☐ SELL ☐ PAIR : ____________

M1 ☐ M5 ☐ M15 ☐ M30 ☐ H1 ☐ H4 ☐ D1 ☐

ENTRY TIME: ____________

ENTRY PRICE: ____________

LOT SIZE: ____________

SPREAD: ____________

PIP GOAL: ____________

TP/SL

TP1: ____________

TP2 : ____________

STOP LOSS : ____________

PATTERN

☐ ____________

☐ ____________

TRADE STRATEGY

☐ ____________

☐ ____________

TRADE RECAP

WIN ☐ LOSS ☐

LIVE TRADE TRACKER

DATE : ______________ BUY ☐ SELL ☐ PAIR : ______________

M1 ☐ M5 ☐ M15 ☐ M30 ☐ H1 ☐ H4 ☐ D1 ☐

ENTRY TIME: ______________

ENTRY PRICE: ______________

LOT SIZE: ______________

SPREAD: ______________

PIP GOAL: ______________

TP/SL

TP1: ______________

TP2 : ______________

STOP LOSS : ______________

PATTERN

☐ ______________

☐ ______________

TRADE STRATEGY

☐ ______________

☐ ______________

TRADE RECAP

WIN ☐ LOSS ☐

LIVE TRADE TRACKER

DATE : ______ BUY ☐ SELL ☐ PAIR : ______

M1 ☐ M5 ☐ M15 ☐ M30 ☐ H1 ☐ H4 ☐ D1 ☐

ENTRY TIME: ______

ENTRY PRICE: ______

LOT SIZE: ______

SPREAD: ______

PIP GOAL: ______

TP/SL

TP1: ______

TP2 : ______

STOP LOSS : ______

PATTERN

☐ ______
☐ ______

TRADE STRATEGY

☐ ______
☐ ______

TRADE RECAP

WIN ☐ LOSS ☐

LIVE TRADE TRACKER

DATE : ____________ BUY ☐ SELL ☐ PAIR : ____________

M1 ☐ M5 ☐ M15 ☐ M30 ☐ H1 ☐ H4 ☐ D1 ☐

ENTRY TIME: ____________

ENTRY PRICE: ____________

LOT SIZE: ____________

SPREAD: ____________

PIP GOAL: ____________

TP/SL

TP1: ____________

TP2 : ____________

STOP LOSS : ____________

PATTERN

☐ ____________

☐ ____________

TRADE RECAP

WIN ☐ LOSS ☐

TRADE STRATEGY

☐ ____________

☐ ____________

LIVE TRADE TRACKER

DATE : ____________ BUY ☐ SELL ☐ PAIR : ____________

M1 ☐ M5 ☐ M15 ☐ M30 ☐ H1 ☐ H4 ☐ D1 ☐

ENTRY TIME: ____________

ENTRY PRICE: ____________

LOT SIZE: ____________

SPREAD: ____________

PIP GOAL: ____________

TP/SL

TP1: ____________

TP2 : ____________

STOP LOSS : ____________

PATTERN

☐ ____________

☐ ____________

TRADE STRATEGY

☐ ____________

☐ ____________

TRADE RECAP

WIN ☐ LOSS ☐

LIVE TRADE TRACKER

DATE : ________ BUY ☐ SELL ☐ PAIR : ________

M1 ☐ M5 ☐ M15 ☐ M30 ☐ H1 ☐ H4 ☐ D1 ☐

ENTRY TIME: ________

ENTRY PRICE: ________

LOT SIZE: ________

SPREAD: ________

PIP GOAL: ________

TP/SL

TP1: ________

TP2 : ________

STOP LOSS : ________

PATTERN

☐ ________

☐ ________

TRADE STRATEGY

☐ ________

☐ ________

TRADE RECAP

WIN ☐ LOSS ☐

LIVE TRADE TRACKER

DATE : ______ BUY ☐ SELL ☐ PAIR : ______

M1 ☐ M5 ☐ M15 ☐ M30 ☐ H1 ☐ H4 ☐ D1 ☐

ENTRY TIME: ______

ENTRY PRICE: ______

LOT SIZE: ______

SPREAD: ______

PIP GOAL: ______

TP/SL

TP1: ______

TP2 : ______

STOP LOSS : ______

PATTERN

☐ ______

☐ ______

TRADE STRATEGY

☐ ______

☐ ______

TRADE RECAP

WIN ☐ LOSS ☐

LIVE TRADE TRACKER

DATE : ____________ BUY ☐ SELL ☐ PAIR : ____________

M1 ☐ M5 ☐ M15 ☐ M30 ☐ H1 ☐ H4 ☐ D1 ☐

ENTRY TIME: ____________

ENTRY PRICE: ____________

LOT SIZE: ____________

SPREAD: ____________

PIP GOAL: ____________

TP/SL

TP1: ____________

TP2 : ____________

STOP LOSS : ____________

PATTERN

☐ ____________

☐ ____________

TRADE STRATEGY

☐ ____________

☐ ____________

TRADE RECAP

WIN ☐ LOSS ☐

LIVE TRADE TRACKER

DATE : ____________ BUY ☐ SELL ☐ PAIR : ____________

M1 ☐ M5 ☐ M15 ☐ M30 ☐ H1 ☐ H4 ☐ D1 ☐

ENTRY TIME: ____________

ENTRY PRICE: ____________

LOT SIZE: ____________

SPREAD: ____________

PIP GOAL: ____________

TP/SL

TP1: ____________

TP2 : ____________

STOP LOSS : ____________

PATTERN

☐ ____________

☐ ____________

TRADE STRATEGY

☐ ____________

☐ ____________

TRADE RECAP

WIN ☐ LOSS ☐

LIVE REFLECTION (51-60)

VIDEO NOTES

TEAM NOTES

BIGGEST WIN

TEACHABLE MOMENT

NOTES

LIVE TRADE TRACKER

DATE : ____________ BUY ☐ SELL ☐ PAIR : ____________

M1 ☐ M5 ☐ M15 ☐ M30 ☐ H1 ☐ H4 ☐ D1 ☐

ENTRY TIME: ____________

ENTRY PRICE: ____________

LOT SIZE: ____________

SPREAD: ____________

PIP GOAL: ____________

TP/SL

TP1: ____________

TP2 : ____________

STOP LOSS : ____________

PATTERN

☐ ____________

☐ ____________

TRADE STRATEGY

☐ ____________

☐ ____________

TRADE RECAP

WIN ☐ LOSS ☐

LIVE TRADE TRACKER

DATE : ____________ BUY ☐ SELL ☐ PAIR : ____________

M1 ☐ M5 ☐ M15 ☐ M30 ☐ H1 ☐ H4 ☐ D1 ☐

ENTRY TIME: ____________

ENTRY PRICE: ____________

LOT SIZE: ____________

SPREAD: ____________

PIP GOAL: ____________

TP/SL

TP1: ____________

TP2 : ____________

STOP LOSS : ____________

PATTERN

☐ ____________

☐ ____________

TRADE STRATEGY

☐ ____________

☐ ____________

TRADE RECAP

WIN ☐ LOSS ☐

LIVE TRADE TRACKER

DATE : ____________ BUY ☐ SELL ☐ PAIR : ____________

M1 ☐ M5 ☐ M15 ☐ M30 ☐ H1 ☐ H4 ☐ D1 ☐

ENTRY TIME: ____________

ENTRY PRICE: ____________

LOT SIZE: ____________

SPREAD: ____________

PIP GOAL: ____________

TP/SL

TP1: ____________

TP2 : ____________

STOP LOSS : ____________

PATTERN

☐ ____________
☐ ____________

TRADE STRATEGY

☐ ____________
☐ ____________

TRADE RECAP

WIN ☐ LOSS ☐

LIVE TRADE TRACKER

DATE : ______ BUY ☐ SELL ☐ PAIR : ______

M1 ☐ M5 ☐ M15 ☐ M30 ☐ H1 ☐ H4 ☐ D1 ☐

ENTRY TIME: ______

ENTRY PRICE: ______

LOT SIZE: ______

SPREAD: ______

PIP GOAL: ______

TRADE RECAP

WIN ☐ LOSS ☐

TP/SL

TP1: ______

TP2 : ______

STOP LOSS : ______

PATTERN

☐ ______

☐ ______

TRADE STRATEGY

☐ ______

☐ ______

LIVE TRADE TRACKER

DATE : ____________ BUY ☐ SELL ☐ PAIR : ____________

M1 ☐ M5 ☐ M15 ☐ M30 ☐ H1 ☐ H4 ☐ D1 ☐

ENTRY TIME: ____________

ENTRY PRICE: ____________

LOT SIZE: ____________

SPREAD: ____________

PIP GOAL: ____________

TP/SL

TP1: ____________

TP2 : ____________

STOP LOSS : ____________

PATTERN

☐ ____________

☐ ____________

TRADE RECAP

WIN ☐ LOSS ☐

TRADE STRATEGY

☐ ____________

☐ ____________

LIVE TRADE TRACKER

DATE : ____________ BUY ☐ SELL ☐ PAIR : ____________

M1 ☐ M5 ☐ M15 ☐ M30 ☐ H1 ☐ H4 ☐ D1 ☐

ENTRY TIME:

ENTRY PRICE:

LOT SIZE:

SPREAD:

PIP GOAL:

TRADE RECAP

WIN ☐ LOSS ☐

TP/SL

TP1:

TP2 :

STOP LOSS :

PATTERN

☐

☐

TRADE STRATEGY

☐

☐

LIVE TRADE TRACKER

DATE : ____________ BUY ☐ SELL ☐ PAIR : ____________

M1 ☐ M5 ☐ M15 ☐ M30 ☐ H1 ☐ H4 ☐ D1 ☐

ENTRY TIME: ____________

ENTRY PRICE: ____________

LOT SIZE: ____________

SPREAD: ____________

PIP GOAL: ____________

TP/SL

TP1: ____________

TP2 : ____________

STOP LOSS : ____________

PATTERN

☐ ____________

☐ ____________

TRADE RECAP

WIN ☐ LOSS ☐

TRADE STRATEGY

☐ ____________

☐ ____________

LIVE TRADE TRACKER

DATE : ______ BUY ☐ SELL ☐ PAIR : ______

M1 ☐ M5 ☐ M15 ☐ M30 ☐ H1 ☐ H4 ☐ D1 ☐

ENTRY TIME: ______

ENTRY PRICE: ______

LOT SIZE: ______

SPREAD: ______

PIP GOAL: ______

TP/SL

TP1: ______

TP2 : ______

STOP LOSS : ______

PATTERN

☐ ______

☐ ______

TRADE STRATEGY

☐ ______

☐ ______

TRADE RECAP

WIN ☐ LOSS ☐

LIVE TRADE TRACKER

DATE : ____________ BUY ☐ SELL ☐ PAIR : ____________

M1 ☐ M5 ☐ M15 ☐ M30 ☐ H1 ☐ H4 ☐ D1 ☐

ENTRY TIME: ____________

ENTRY PRICE: ____________

LOT SIZE: ____________

SPREAD: ____________

PIP GOAL: ____________

TP/SL

TP1: ____________

TP2 : ____________

STOP LOSS : ____________

PATTERN

☐ ____________

☐ ____________

TRADE RECAP

WIN ☐ LOSS ☐

TRADE STRATEGY

☐ ____________

☐ ____________

LIVE TRADE TRACKER

DATE : ______ BUY ☐ SELL ☐ PAIR : ______

M1 ☐ M5 ☐ M15 ☐ M30 ☐ H1 ☐ H4 ☐ D1 ☐

ENTRY TIME: ______

ENTRY PRICE: ______

LOT SIZE: ______

SPREAD: ______

PIP GOAL: ______

TP/SL

TP1: ______

TP2 : ______

STOP LOSS : ______

PATTERN

☐ ______

☐ ______

TRADE STRATEGY

☐ ______

☐ ______

TRADE RECAP

WIN ☐ LOSS ☐

LIVE REFLECTION (61-70)

VIDEO NOTES

TEAM NOTES

BIGGEST WIN

TEACHABLE MOMENT

NOTES

LIVE TRADE TRACKER

DATE : ______ BUY ☐ SELL ☐ PAIR : ______

M1 ☐ M5 ☐ M15 ☐ M30 ☐ H1 ☐ H4 ☐ D1 ☐

ENTRY TIME: ______

ENTRY PRICE: ______

LOT SIZE: ______

SPREAD: ______

PIP GOAL: ______

TP/SL

TP1: ______

TP2 : ______

STOP LOSS : ______

PATTERN

☐ ______
☐ ______

TRADE RECAP

WIN ☐ LOSS ☐

______

TRADE STRATEGY

☐ ______
☐ ______

LIVE TRADE TRACKER

DATE : ____________ BUY ☐ SELL ☐ PAIR : ____________

M1 ☐ M5 ☐ M15 ☐ M30 ☐ H1 ☐ H4 ☐ D1 ☐

ENTRY TIME:

ENTRY PRICE:

LOT SIZE:

SPREAD:

PIP GOAL:

TP/SL

TP1:

TP2 :

STOP LOSS :

PATTERN

☐

☐

TRADE RECAP

WIN ☐ LOSS ☐

TRADE STRATEGY

☐

☐

LIVE TRADE TRACKER

DATE : ____________ BUY ☐ SELL ☐ PAIR : ____________

M1 ☐ M5 ☐ M15 ☐ M30 ☐ H1 ☐ H4 ☐ D1 ☐

ENTRY TIME: ____________

ENTRY PRICE: ____________

LOT SIZE: ____________

SPREAD: ____________

PIP GOAL: ____________

TP/SL

TP1: ____________

TP2 : ____________

STOP LOSS : ____________

PATTERN

☐ ____________

☐ ____________

TRADE STRATEGY

☐ ____________

☐ ____________

TRADE RECAP

WIN ☐ LOSS ☐

LIVE TRADE TRACKER

DATE : ____________ BUY ☐ SELL ☐ PAIR : ____________

M1 ☐ M5 ☐ M15 ☐ M30 ☐ H1 ☐ H4 ☐ D1 ☐

ENTRY TIME: ____________

ENTRY PRICE: ____________

LOT SIZE: ____________

SPREAD: ____________

PIP GOAL: ____________

TP/SL

TP1: ____________

TP2 : ____________

STOP LOSS : ____________

PATTERN

☐ ____________

☐ ____________

TRADE STRATEGY

☐ ____________

☐ ____________

TRADE RECAP

WIN ☐ LOSS ☐

LIVE TRADE TRACKER

DATE : ______ BUY ☐ SELL ☐ PAIR : ______

M1 ☐ M5 ☐ M15 ☐ M30 ☐ H1 ☐ H4 ☐ D1 ☐

ENTRY TIME: ______

ENTRY PRICE: ______

LOT SIZE: ______

SPREAD: ______

PIP GOAL: ______

TP/SL

TP1: ______

TP2 : ______

STOP LOSS : ______

PATTERN

☐ ______

☐ ______

TRADE RECAP

WIN ☐ LOSS ☐

TRADE STRATEGY

☐ ______

☐ ______

LIVE TRADE TRACKER

DATE : ________ BUY ☐ SELL ☐ PAIR : ________

M1 ☐ M5 ☐ M15 ☐ M30 ☐ H1 ☐ H4 ☐ D1 ☐

ENTRY TIME: ________

ENTRY PRICE: ________

LOT SIZE: ________

SPREAD: ________

PIP GOAL: ________

TP/SL

TP1: ________

TP2 : ________

STOP LOSS : ________

PATTERN

☐ ________

☐ ________

TRADE RECAP

WIN ☐ LOSS ☐

TRADE STRATEGY

☐ ________

☐ ________

LIVE TRADE TRACKER

DATE : ____________ BUY ☐ SELL ☐ PAIR : ____________

M1 ☐ M5 ☐ M15 ☐ M30 ☐ H1 ☐ H4 ☐ D1 ☐

ENTRY TIME: ____________

ENTRY PRICE: ____________

LOT SIZE: ____________

SPREAD: ____________

PIP GOAL: ____________

TP/SL

TP1: ____________

TP2 : ____________

STOP LOSS : ____________

PATTERN

☐ ____________

☐ ____________

TRADE RECAP

WIN ☐ LOSS ☐

TRADE STRATEGY

☐ ____________

☐ ____________

LIVE TRADE TRACKER

DATE : ______ BUY ☐ SELL ☐ PAIR : ______

M1 ☐ M5 ☐ M15 ☐ M30 ☐ H1 ☐ H4 ☐ D1 ☐

ENTRY TIME: ______

ENTRY PRICE: ______

LOT SIZE: ______

SPREAD: ______

PIP GOAL: ______

TP/SL

TP1: ______

TP2 : ______

STOP LOSS : ______

PATTERN

☐ ______

☐ ______

TRADE STRATEGY

☐ ______

☐ ______

TRADE RECAP

WIN ☐ LOSS ☐

LIVE TRADE TRACKER

DATE : ____________ BUY ☐ SELL ☐ PAIR : ____________

M1 ☐ M5 ☐ M15 ☐ M30 ☐ H1 ☐ H4 ☐ D1 ☐

TP/SL

TP1: ____________

TP2 : ____________

STOP LOSS : ____________

ENTRY TIME: ____________

ENTRY PRICE: ____________

LOT SIZE: ____________

SPREAD: ____________

PIP GOAL: ____________

PATTERN

☐ ____________

☐ ____________

TRADE STRATEGY

☐ ____________

☐ ____________

TRADE RECAP

WIN ☐ LOSS ☐

LIVE TRADE TRACKER

DATE : ______ BUY ☐ SELL ☐ PAIR : ______

M1 ☐ M5 ☐ M15 ☐ M30 ☐ H1 ☐ H4 ☐ D1 ☐

ENTRY TIME: ______

ENTRY PRICE: ______

LOT SIZE: ______

SPREAD: ______

PIP GOAL: ______

TP/SL

TP1: ______

TP2 : ______

STOP LOSS : ______

PATTERN

☐ ______

☐ ______

TRADE STRATEGY

☐ ______

☐ ______

TRADE RECAP

WIN ☐ LOSS ☐

LIVE REFLECTION (71-80)

VIDEO NOTES

TEAM NOTES

BIGGEST WIN

TEACHABLE MOMENT

NOTES

TRADE RESOURCES

CALENDAR

forexfactory.com

CURRENCY/STRENGTH METER

forexfactory.com
livecharts.co.uk

NEWS

bloomberg.com (use this resource for stocks & currency)
cnbc.com
cnn.com
investing.com
tradingeconomics.com

PIPS

babypips.com

TRADING TERMS

forex-trader.com
forextime.com/education/forex-glossary

TRENDS

tradingview.com

YOUR WINNER'S INVITATION

WIN WITH US

Do you see your
PROFIT-ABILITY? I can!

I'd love the privilege to coach
you to your *Winning* Place

Follow me @winnerscoach
on Instagram & Facebook
for more Winning Tips

*If you would like to explore
trading with me & our Blue Skies
Trading Group,* visit
blueskiestradinggroup.com

On the following page there's room
for you to write the names & contact
information of five individuals that you
would like to extend this winner's
invitation with.

When done, email
winnerscoach.dme@gmail.com
for next steps

PROSPECT SHEET

Record the names of at least three people you'd like
to join our team of Forex Traders.

1 ______________________________

EMAIL ☐ IN-PERSON ☐ PHONE ☐ TEXT ☐

2 ______________________________

EMAIL ☐ IN-PERSON ☐ PHONE ☐ TEXT ☐

3 ______________________________

EMAIL ☐ IN-PERSON ☐ PHONE ☐ TEXT ☐

4 ______________________________

EMAIL ☐ IN-PERSON ☐ PHONE ☐ TEXT ☐

5 ______________________________

EMAIL ☐ IN-PERSON ☐ PHONE ☐ TEXT ☐

ABOUT THE AUTHOR

Winner's Coach Rev. Donna Edward is a multi-faceted business professional with 25+ years of experience as a marketplace and ministry expert who equips and empowers people. With a passion for entrepreneurship, philanthropy and teaching others how to develop a winning mentality, this world-renowned leader is also a CA Real Estate Salesperson/investor who uses multiple platforms including radio and television to train and mentor forward-thinking leaders across the country and abroad. Her accolades include Best-Selling Author, and Certified Professional Coach.

Expertise

1. Success Coaching
2. Relationship Mediation (Marriage, Divorce, Families & Aging Parents)
3. Ministry & Marketplace Leadership
4. Non-Profit Team Building
5. Life Strategy Development
6. Personal Imaging
7. Branding

As a member partner of *Blue Skies Trading Group LLC.*, and celebrated for establishing *G.G.N.* (The Godly Girls Network) - a Global Non-Profit Organization, *F.A.C.T.* (Families Against Child Trafficking), *Life Guide Coaches LLC.*, and *The Winner's Coaching Center*, Coach Donna continues to innovate programs, products, and services that groom men and women for greatness.

Made in the USA
Monee, IL
05 November 2026

67811370R10090